📖 DK READERS

DISCARD

Level 2

Dinosaur Dinners
Fire Fighter!
Bugs! Bugs! Bugs!
Slinky, Scaly Snakes!
Animal Hospital
The Little Ballerina
Munching, Crunching, Sniffing,
   and Snooping
The Secret Life of Trees
Winking, Blinking, Wiggling,
   and Waggling
Astronaut: Living in Space
Twisters

The Story of Pocahontas
Horse Show
Survivors: The Night the Titanic
   Sank
Eruption! The Story of Volcanoes
The Story of Columbus
Journey of a Humpback Whale
Amazing Buildings
LEGO: Castle Under Attack
LEGO: Rocket Rescue
¡Insectos! en español
Ice Skating Stars

Level 3

Spacebusters: The Race to the Moon
Beastly Tales
Shark Attack!
Titanic
Invaders from Outer Space
Plants Bite Back!
Time Traveler
Bermuda Triangle
Tiger Tales
Spies
Terror on the Amazon
Disasters at Sea
The Story of Anne Frank
Movie Magic

Abraham Lincoln: Lawyer,
   Leader, Legend
George Washington: Soldier,
   Hero, President
Extreme Sports
LEGO: Mission to the Arctic
NFL: Super Bowl Heroes
MLB: Home Run Heroes: Big
   Mac, Sammy, and Junior
MLB: Roberto Clemente
MLB: World Series Heroes
The Big Dinosaur Dig
Space Heroes: Amazing Astronauts
MLB: Home Run Heroes
MLB: Record Breakers

Level 4

Days of the Knights
Volcanoes
Secrets of the Mummies
Pirates: Raiders of the High Seas
Horse Heroes
Micro Monsters
Going for Gold!
Extreme Machines
Flying Ace: The Story of
   Amelia Earhart
Free at Last! The Story of Martin
   Luther King, Jr.
First Flight: The Story of the Wright
   Brothers

The Incredible Hulk's Book of
Strength
The Story of the Incredible Hulk
MLB: The Story of the New York
   Yankees
JLA Readers Level 4: Batman's Guide
   to the Universe
JLA Readers Level 4: Superman's
   Guide to the Universe
NFL's Greatest Upsets
NFL: Rumbling Running Backs
LEGO: Race for Survival
NFL: Super Bowl!

A Note to Parents and Teachers

DK READERS is a compelling program for beginning readers, designed in conjunction with leading literacy experts, including Dr. Linda Gambrell, director of the Eugene T. Moore School of Education, Clemson University, and past president of the National Reading Conference.

Beautiful illustrations and superb full-color photographs combine with engaging, easy-to-read stories to offer a fresh approach to each subject in the series. Each DK READER is guaranteed to capture a child's interest while developing his or her reading skills, general knowledge, and love of reading.

The four levels of DK READERS are aimed at different reading abilities, enabling you to choose the books that are exactly right for your children:

Level 1 – Beginning to read
Level 2 – Beginning to read alone
Level 3 – Reading alone
Level 4 – Proficient readers

The "normal" age at which a child begins to read can be anywhere from three to eight years old, so these levels are only a general guideline.

No matter which level you select, you can be sure that you are helping your child learn to read, then read to learn!

DK

LONDON, NEW YORK, MELBOURNE,
MUNICH, and DELHI

Senior Editor Beth Sutinis
Senior Art Editor Michelle Baxter
Publisher Chuck Lang
Creative Director Tina Vaughan
Production Chris Avgherinos

Reading Consultant
Linda Gambrell, Ph.D.

Produced by
Shoreline Publishing Group
Editorial Director James Buckley, Jr.
Art Director Tom Carling
Carling Design, Inc.

Produced in partnership and licensed by
Major League Baseball Properties, Inc.
Vice President of Publishing
Don Hintze

First American Edition, 2003
03 04 05 10 9 8 7 6 5 4 3 2 1

Published in the United States by DK Publishing, Inc.
375 Hudson St., New York, NY 10014

Published in Great Britain by Dorling Kindersley Limited

A catalog record is available from the Library of Congress

0-7894-9845-6 (PB)
0-7894-9844-8 (HC)

Color reproduction by Colourscan, Singapore
Printed and bound in China by L Rex Printing Co., Ltd.

Photography credits:
All photo courtesy of and copyright MLB Photos except
the following: AP/Wide World:12, 15tr, 18t, 24b, 25b;
Courtesy Ebbets Field Flannels: 29; Library of Congress: 7tr;
Transcendental Graphics: 7b, 10t, 11t, 22, 22, 28t; The Flag
Institute, Chester, UK: 28b.

Discover more at
www.dk.com

Contents

DK READERS

PROFICIENT READERS 4

MAJOR LEAGUE BASEBALL™

THE WORLD OF
BASEBALL

Written by James Buckley, Jr.

DK Publishing, Inc.

A baseball world

Although baseball is known as America's "National Pastime," it is played all around the world. Since the first games were played in New Jersey in 1839, baseball has spread to every part of the globe.

At a Major League game, you might see a scene like this: A pitcher from Japan gets the sign from his

Sayonara
In a Major League game played in Tokyo, Japan, in 2001, Benny Agbayani of the Mets slugged a game-winning grand slam home run.

Early days
The IBAF was founded in 1938. It has helped put on tournaments that crown world champions.

The baseball "pins" on this world map show countries that are members of the International Baseball Federation (IBAF). Central America, the Caribbean, Europe, and Asia have the most members. The IBAF helps train new players and helps countries develop national team programs.

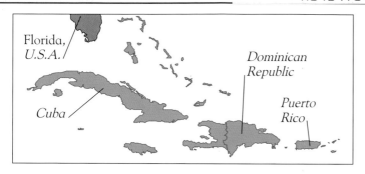

Florida, U.S.A.

Cuba

Dominican Republic

Puerto Rico

Island ball
The countries shown on this map send more players to the Majors than any other nations. The countries are located in the Caribbean Sea just south of the state of Florida (upper left of map).

catcher, a native of Puerto Rico. The batter, who is from the Dominican Republic, lofts a fly ball to the outfield, where a player from Cuba circles under it.

In 2003, one-quarter of Major Leaguers were from outside the United States.

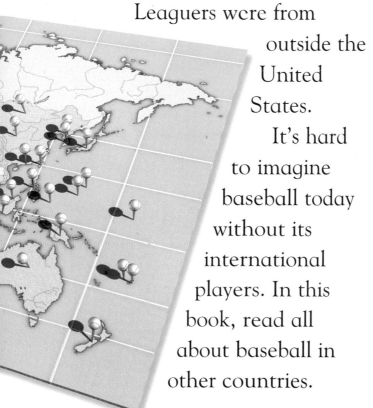

It's hard to imagine baseball today without its international players. In this book, read all about baseball in other countries.

International All-Stars
At the Major League All-Star Game in Milwaukee in 2002, 24 players on the two teams were born outside the United States. That was the highest total ever for the game also known as the Midsummer Classic.

5

Birth of the Majors
The first pro league was the National Association, which first played in 1871.

On the road
This photo shows the players on the 1889 world tour posing on the Sphinx statue in Egypt.

International game
Major League Baseball began in America in the 1870s. Less than 20 years later, pro players were taking the game to the world.

In 1889, star pitcher Albert Spalding organized a world tour. About 24 pro players went on the journey.

When the trip ended the players had left behind rule books and new fans. They played in Australia, inspiring the formation of teams "down under." They played in Egypt, posing for a famous picture on the Sphinx. Europe saw baseball for the first time in Italy.

In the early 1900s, tours continued. An all-star team went to Japan, where the game was already well known (see page 10).

England is the home of a game called cricket, which some people think is a relative of baseball. England welcomed a baseball tour in 1914. Even King George V came out to meet the players and watch a game.

Meanwhile, some of the first foreign players began to come into the Major Leagues.

Pro Scot
Scotland native Jim McCormick pitched from 1878 to 1887. He once won 45 games in one season!

Good show!
King George V of England watched the White Sox and Giants play this 1914 exhibition game in Great Britain.

Go Guam!
This team of U.S. soldiers were champions of a league on this remote Pacific island.

Fly boys
On their base in the Far East, these members of an Army Air Force (AAF) team spoke to the troops over the radio set at their feet.

In the 1940s, World War II had a terrible effect on many countries. One good result was that American soldiers took their national game with them as they fought around the world. Soldiers storming the beach on D-Day in June, 1944, carried baseballs and bats. Special Army teams, which often included Major League stars, such as Joe DiMaggio, played for thrilled servicemen on Army bases.

By the 1950s, national leagues were established in Japan, Mexico, and several Caribbean countries, including Cuba. In the 1960s and 1970s, the continued growth of international baseball led to a call for baseball to become an Olympic sport.

In 1984, at the Los Angeles Olympics, a special exhibition was held. By 1992, baseball had become a regular part of the Games.

Japan won the gold in 1984, and Cuba won in 1992 and 1996. America's top amateur players made up a team that won the gold medal in 2000 in Australia.

Let's take a spin around the globe and visit the key baseball countries. Baseball has now become the "*inter*national pastime."

Future stars
Future Major League stars Tino Martinez and Jim Abbott (arms raised) greet fellow future star Rafael Palmeiro (29) during the 1984 Olympic baseball tournament held in Los Angeles, California.

First in U.S.
In 1965, pitcher Masanori Murakami became the first Major League player from Japan.

 # Japan

Baseball has been played in Japan nearly as long as it has been played in America. The first teams were formed by American missionaries in the 1870s. By 1908, Japanese college teams were good enough to beat visiting American collegians.

Other American visitors included Major League stars. The Chicago White Sox traveled east in 1913. Ty Cobb came over in 1928 to help teach Japanese players his hitting secrets.

In 1934, a large group of Major Leaguers played a series of exhibition games in Japan. Babe Ruth, Lou Gehrig, Al Simmons, Lefty Gomez, and Jimmie Foxx headed up the all-star lineup.

Play ball!
This 1963 photo shows Korokuen Stadium, then home to the Tokyo Giants.

In one game, a young Japanese player showed what his countrymen could do. Though only 18, Eiji Sawamura struck out Ruth, Gehrig, and Foxx in order.

In 1936, the country's first pro league was started. It ended because of World War II in 1941. After the war, more American stars visited to revive interest in the game. By 1950, a new pro league had started. Today, the league has 12 teams that draw millions of fans.

Babe goes East Babe Ruth (he's the "big kid") was one of many Major League stars who went to Japan in the first half of the century. The Babe led a tour of the country in 1934 that included several future Hall of Fame players.

Champs!
American Tom O'Malley is at the center of this celebration in 1995. After winning the Japan Series that year, the Yakult Swallows celebrated. It was the team's first title since 1978.

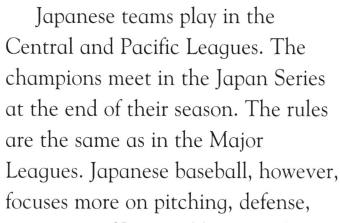

Japanese teams play in the Central and Pacific Leagues. The champions meet in the Japan Series at the end of their season. The rules are the same as in the Major Leagues. Japanese baseball, however, focuses more on pitching, defense, and bunting than on big hits like the home run.

Just as in America, fans follow their favorite stars with great devotion. There are many magazines and newspapers in Japan about baseball. During games, fans cheer almost constantly and sing songs.

Unlike in America, Japanese teams are named for the companies that own them. The Nippon Ham Fighters, for instance, are not named for battling pigs, but for the food company that owns the team. The most famous and successful team is the Tokyo Yomiuri Giants.

Some American players have gone to Japan to play ball. Warren Cromartie led the Central League in hitting in 1990. Slugger Cecil Fielder had success in Japan before his great Major League career. Tom O'Malley was the Central League MVP in 1995, a rare feat for a foreigner.

However, the big news in Japanese baseball lately has been the talented pitchers and batters from the Far East who come to play in the Major Leagues.

Swing away
Japanese teams use uniforms similar to Major League teams, but add company logos on shirts and helmets.

In the news
Japanese fans read colorful magazines about their favorite teams.

In 1965, Masanori Murakami was the first player from Japan to join the Majors. However, it was not until 1995, when Hideo Nomo entered the league, that Americans believed Japanese players could make it in the U.S. Nomo had been a top pitcher in Japan, leading the Pacific League in wins four times. He joined the Los Angeles Dodgers in 1995 and earned Rookie of the Year honors. He led the National League in strikeouts.

Fans back home woke up early to watch Nomo's games, which were all broadcast live in Japan. While Nomo continued to excel, his success paved the way for a wave of Japanese players, most of whom were pitchers.

In the middle
Shigetoshi Hasegawa's specialty is middle relief, pitching the innings from when the starting pitcher finishes until the closer begins.

Time change
They called it "Nomo-mania" when Japanese fans followed Nomo in the U.S. A 7 P.M. game in Los Angeles was on at 11 A.M. in Japan.

Shigetoshi Hasegawa has been an ace middle reliever for the Angels and Mariners. Hideki Irabu pitched for the New York Yankees and Texas Rangers before returning to pitch in Japan in 2003. Kazuhisa Ishii is a key part of the Los Angeles Dodgers' starting rotation.

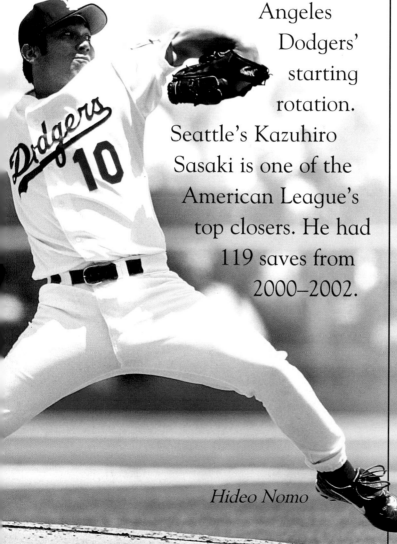

Seattle's Kazuhiro Sasaki is one of the American League's top closers. He had 119 saves from 2000–2002.

Hideo Nomo

Oh, my!
Japan produced the greatest home run hitter of all time. Sadaharu Oh smacked 868 home runs in his pro career in Japan.

Close the door
Relief pitchers who are called on to finish off a win for a team, often in tough situations, are called "closers" or "stoppers." Most teams rely on one top pitcher to be their closer.

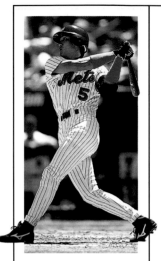

Lucky find
Mets outfielder Tsuyoshi Shinjo became the first Japanese player to get a hit in the World Series as a member of the San Francisco Giants in 2003.

New star
Yankees star Hideki Matsui is known as "Godzilla."

The most famous, and perhaps the best, Japanese player in the Major Leagues is known the world over by one name: Ichiro.

Ichiro Suzuki was the top hitter in Japan for seven seasons, winning batting title after batting title. Many wondered if his talent would translate to the game in America.

In 2001, he became the first non-pitcher to join the Majors from Japan. He did more than just join the Seattle Mariners—he took America by storm.

Ichiro became the first Japanese-born player to win a batting title. He had a .350 average! His 242 hits were the second-most all-time for a player in his first Major League season. He received more votes for the All-Star Game than any other player. A strong-armed outfielder, he also won a Gold Glove for his great fielding skills.

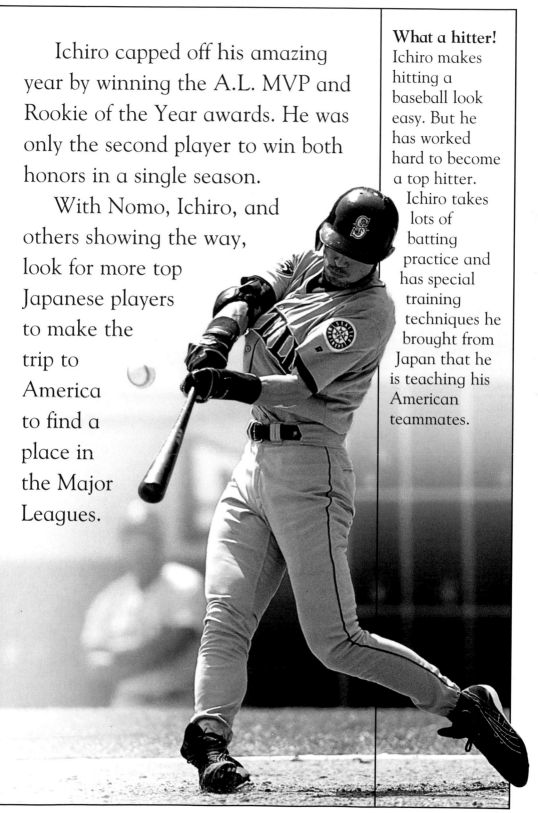

Ichiro capped off his amazing year by winning the A.L. MVP and Rookie of the Year awards. He was only the second player to win both honors in a single season.

With Nomo, Ichiro, and others showing the way, look for more top Japanese players to make the trip to America to find a place in the Major Leagues.

What a hitter!
Ichiro makes hitting a baseball look easy. But he has worked hard to become a top hitter. Ichiro takes lots of batting practice and has special training techniques he brought from Japan that he is teaching his American teammates.

Mexico

America's closest neighbor to the south was one of the first countries outside the U.S. to play baseball. By the early 1900s, a league had formed with teams in several cities.

In 1946, the Mexican League challenged the Major Leagues.

Hangin' out
These players wait their turn at bat during a Mexican League game in 1948.

Beisbol
Mexico sends its top players to its national team for international competitions such as the Pan Am Games and the Olympics. *Beisbol* is the Spanish word for baseball.

The league offered American players big money to play in Mexico. Sal Maglie and Mickey Owen are among a handful of stars who headed south. Negro League stars Josh Gibson and Satchel Paige also were lured to Mexico. But the plan failed when players later left.

Today, the Mexican League is a strong again, with 16 teams playing a 65-game schedule. The most famous teams include the Diablos Rojos (Red Devils) and the Tigres (Tigers). The Diablos were the 2002 champions.

In 1957, a team from Monterrey, Mexico, became the first team from outside the U.S. to win the Little League World Series. Forty years later, a team from Guadalupe, Mexico, also won that famous championship.

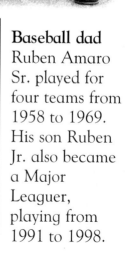

"The Barber"
After leaving the Mexican League, Sal Maglie was a star pitcher for the Yankees and Dodgers.

Baseball dad
Ruben Amaro Sr. played for four teams from 1958 to 1969. His son Ruben Jr. also became a Major Leaguer, playing from 1991 to 1998.

Mexico in Milwaukee
Teddy Higuera pitched for the Brewers from 1985 to 1994.

Big hitter
Third baseman Vinny Castilla has smashed more than 40 homers in a season three times.

The great legacy of Mexican baseball has led to many players bringing their game to the Major Leagues. The first was Mel Almada, an outfielder who played in the U.S. from 1933 to 1939.

Other Mexican-born big-leaguers include Vinny Castilla, Ismael Valdes, Juan Acevedo, Erubiel Durazo, and Benji Gil.

But the most famous Mexican player ever was a lefthanded pitcher known, like Ichiro, by one name only: Fernando.

In 1981, young Fernando Valenzuela earned a spot on the Dodgers' roster. He stunned the baseball world by going 10–0 to start the year. He made the All-Star team, helped the Dodgers win the World Series, and became the first rookie ever to win the Cy Young Award as the N.L.'s top pitcher.

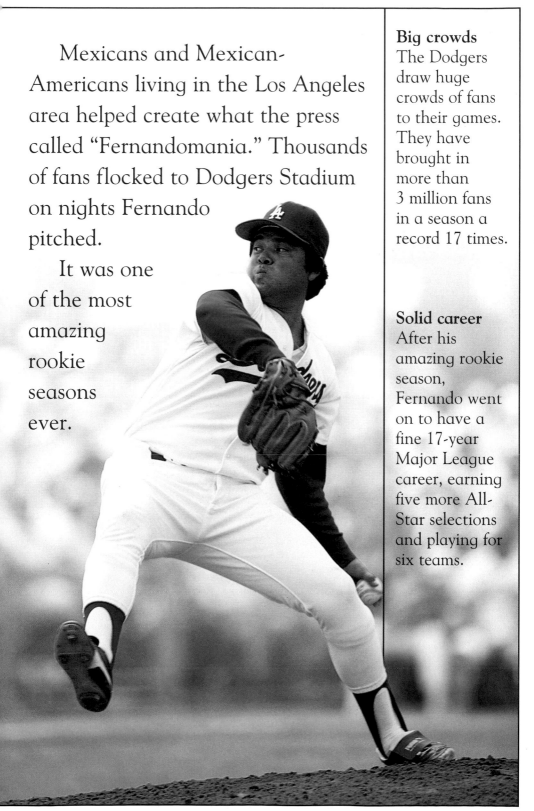

Mexicans and Mexican-Americans living in the Los Angeles area helped create what the press called "Fernandomania." Thousands of fans flocked to Dodgers Stadium on nights Fernando pitched.

It was one of the most amazing rookie seasons ever.

Big crowds
The Dodgers draw huge crowds of fans to their games. They have brought in more than 3 million fans in a season a record 17 times.

Solid career
After his amazing rookie season, Fernando went on to have a fine 17-year Major League career, earning five more All-Star selections and playing for six teams.

Cuba

Cuba may be a small island, but it has made a big impact on the baseball world. Its players have been a part of the Majors almost since the beginning. Teams from Cuba have won numerous Caribbean World Series titles, and its national team has been the world's best for decades.

Early team
This photo from the early 1900s shows an unnamed amateur team from Cuba. Note the early model of the catcher's mask at the bottom center.

American sailors and soldiers probably brought the game to Cuba, perhaps as early

as 1866. Five years later, Esteban Bellan and Emilio Sabourin of Cuba became the first players from Latin America in the Majors.

In 1898, U.S. military forces took over Cuba and helped baseball become more popular on the island. Pro and amateur leagues grew and many top players came to the U.S. to play.

In 1911, Rafael Almeida and Armando Marsans signed to play with Cincinnati. The move was controversial. At the time, many baseball owners refused to hire minorities for their teams.

Sailor ball
This 1920s scene shows U.S. sailors watching a game at Guantanamo Bay, Cuba, which is still a major U.S. naval base.

Finding a way
Almeida and Marsans were called "Spanish" and thus avoided baseball's ban on black players. Other teams wouldn't sign Cubans, but they were welcomed in the Negro Leagues.

The boss bats
Cuban leader
Fidel Castro
had been a top
amateur pitcher
who may have
tried out for
the Yankees.

The best?
In 1977, all-
around star
Martin Dihigo
was the first
Cuban player
named to the
Hall of Fame.

In the 1950s, several Major League teams held spring training in Cuba. And minor league teams based in Cuba played in American leagues.

In 1959, a revolution led by Fidel Castro changed Cuba in many ways, including Cuban baseball. Castro's revolution made Cuba a socialist country. Pro sports were banned, but as amateurs, Cuban players were still among the best. Castro's and the government's support was important to the sport's continued success.

Cuban teams regularly won international tournaments such as the Pan Am Games and the Caribbean World Series. When baseball was added to the Olympics, Cuba won gold medals in 1988, 1992, and 1996.

An important milestone in Cuban baseball came in 1999.

Until then, no American players had visited Cuba since 1960. But in 1999, the Baltimore Orioles traveled to Havana to play the Cuban national team. The Cubans later went to play a game in Baltimore, another historic first. The teams split the "series," each winning on the road.

Big Red
Tony Perez was a top RBI man for the Cincinnati Reds. He helped the team win two World Series. Perez was elected to the Hall of Fame in 2000.

Golden day
Omar Linares and Orestes Kindelan of Cuba wear 1996 Olympic gold medals.

Steady star
Born in Havana, Cuba, first baseman Rafael Palmeiro is one of baseball's steadiest sluggers. He has hit more home runs than any other Cuban-born Major Leaguer.

Batting champ
Tony Oliva won three batting titles in the 1960s, including his rookie year, 1964.

In recent years, some Cubans have escaped from their home country in order to reach America and gain more freedom. Sometimes they have had to go to great lengths and brave dangers to reach America. Their skills and success show that Cuban baseball is alive and well.

Texas Rangers first baseman Rafael Palmeiro is one of baseball's most consistent home-run hitters. He hit 35 or more home runs in eight straight seasons (1995–2002).

Pitcher Orlando Hernandez survived a dangerous boat journey to escape from Cuba. He then signed with the Yankees and helped them win three World Series.

Jose Canseco was the A.L. Most Valuable Player in 1988 when he became the first player with 40 home runs and 40 stolen bases in the same season.

Rey Ordoñez is one of the best-fielding shortstops in the game. Pitcher Jose Contreras hopes to follow the success of Hernandez.

Cuba is still a closed society, cut off from the U.S. by federal law, but the players who get out are continuing a baseball tradition that is more than 100 years old.

Big O
In 2003, Cuban pitcher Orlando Hernandez was traded from the Yankees to the Montreal Expos.

40–40
Jose Canseco combined speed and power to star for seven teams.

Say hey!
Willie Mays was one of many top Major League stars who played winter ball in Puerto Rico. Here the great Giants star slides into third base for the Santurce team.

Puerto Rico

Like Cuba, Puerto Rico is a Caribbean island with a rich baseball tradition. Also as in Cuba, American soldiers brought the sport to the island. The 1898 Spanish-American War made Puerto Rico a part of the United States.

The island now is called a "commonwealth." Puerto Rico votes in U.S. national elections but does not have all the rights that a state does.

By the middle of the 20th century, baseball was a popular game in Puerto Rico. The first Puerto Rican in the Major Leagues was Hiram Bithorn who joined the Chicago Cubs in 1942.

In the 1950s, a popular Puerto Rican winter league attracted many U.S. stars. Top players such as Willie Mays and Whitey Ford stayed in shape and earned money playing in Puerto Rico.

Working men
Most of today's Major Leaguers concentrate on baseball year-round. In earlier days, however, some players had offseason jobs. Hall of Fame catcher Yogi Berra worked in a men's clothing store.

Famous jersey
Roberto Clemente (next page) wore a jersey like this one. His team was called the Cangrejeros, which means "crabbers."

A real hero
Clemente cared deeply for his people and worked hard to help those in need. In 1972, just a few months after getting his 3,000th career hit, there was a terrible earthquake in Nicaragua. While flying there with relief supplies, Clemente was killed in a plane crash.

Honoring his work
Each year, Major League Baseball gives the Roberto Clemente Award to a player who combines great skills on the field with great caring off it.

In 1955, the greatest Puerto Rican player ever made it to the Major Leagues. Over the next 17 seasons, Roberto Clemente would showcase his talents and help open the doors for hundreds more of his fellow Latin American ballplayers.

Clemente grew up playing baseball with a table leg for a bat and a milk carton for a glove. He joined adult teams as a teenager. His great skills caught the attention of scouts, who signed him for the Majors.

He helped the Pittsburgh Pirates win the World Series in 1960, and, in 1961, he became the first Hispanic batting champion. (He won again in 1967.) In 1966, he was named the N.L. MVP.

In 1971, Pittsburgh won the Series again and Clemente was named Series MVP. He was elected to the Hall of Fame in 1973 following his tragic death.

"Baby Bull" Hall of Famer Orlando Cepeda earned that nickname for his powerful swing. He clubbed 379 home runs from 1958 to 1974.

Brother act The Alomar brothers, Roberto and Sandy Jr., followed in the Major League footsteps of their father, Sandy Sr.

31

Multitalented
Along with being one of the A.L.'s top hitters, Bernie Williams is also a very talented classical guitarist who has performed on stage.

While supporting its own popular league, Puerto Rico continues to send great players to the Majors. Catcher Ivan Rodriguez has won 10 Gold Gloves and is considered perhaps the finest defensive catcher of all time. Texas Rangers outfielder Juan Gonzalez is one of baseball's greatest sluggers.

He was named the A.L. MVP in 1996 and 1998.

Centerfielder Bernie Williams of the New York Yankees has been a key part of the great Yankees teams of recent years. He has helped them win four World Series titles since 1996.

Toronto's Carlos Delgado smacked 250 home runs from 1996 to 2002, with a high of 44 in 1999.

Brothers Bengie and Jose Molina, both catchers, helped the Angels win the 2002 World Series.

To show how popular the game continues to be in Puerto Rico, Major League Baseball arranged to have the Montreal Expos play 22 games on the island during the 2003 season. Puerto Ricans were thrilled to see some of the best players in the game.

Going deep
His nickname is "Juan Gone." Juan Gonzalez earned that name by smashing 40 or more home runs in five different seasons.

Heading south
Among the teams Puerto Rican fans will see play in their country in 2003 are the Mets, Marlins, Reds, Rangers, Cubs, Braves, and the 2003 champion Angels.

Island half
The Dominican Republic is a nation located on the eastern half of a Caribbean island called Hispaniola. Haiti is the nation on the western half.

Ozzie II
Ozzie Virgil Jr. followed his father into the Major Leagues. Ozzie Jr. was an All-Star catcher while playing for the Phillies and Braves.

Dominican Republic

Though it is one of the smallest countries in Latin America, the Dominican Republic is a huge part of Major League Baseball.

Cuban players first brought baseball to the D.R., as the country is known, in the late 1800s. American soldiers arrived in 1916 and helped popularize the game.

By the 1930s, a pro league had been formed and top players from around the Caribbean came to play. In 1948, the Dominican national team won the Caribbean baseball championship. A national organization was formed to help the sport grow. In 1956, that organization's efforts paid off when Ozzie Virgil became the first Dominican player to join the M.L.B.

34

Juan great pitcher

Juan great pitcher
Fireballing righthander Juan Marichal was one of the top pitchers of the 1960s. Famous for his high leg kick, he won 243 games in his Hall of Fame career.

Others soon joined him in making the trip from the D.R. to the U.S., including Manny Mota, Juan Marichal, and the Alou brothers.

Felipe, Matty, and Jesus Alou made history in 1963 by becoming the first trio of brothers to play in the same outfield, for the San Francisco Giants.

In a pinch
Until Lenny Harris broke his record in 2002, Manny Mota was the all-time career leader in pinch hits, with 150. Manny now works as a coach for the Dodgers.

Sweet swing
Manny Ramirez is one of baseball's best all-around hitters. He has seven seasons with an average above .300, including an A.L.-leading .349 in 2002. He also has six seasons with 33 or more home runs. His 165 RBI in 1999 is one of the highest single-season totals ever.

Large sugar companies often sponsor teams in the D.R. The center of the sugar industry is the small town of San Pedro de Macoris. Thanks to the company teams, that village is the center of baseball in the Dominican Republic.

Dozens of players from San Pedro de Macoris have made it to the Majors. Many Major League teams have created baseball academies and training camps in the area that scout new players and help young players develop.

The Dominican Republic is, in many places, very poor. The impact of the support from baseball has become important to the nation. As in the United States, young Dominican athletes dream of growing up and making "The Show."

Lately, the greatest player from the island has been

Sammy Sosa, the Chicago Cubs slugger. Sosa had at least 49 homers five seasons in a row (1998 through 2002). In 2003, he became the first Dominican player to top 500 home runs for his career.

Shortstop City
The little town of San Pedro de Macoris has produced many shortstops, including Tony Fernandez, who played 16 Major League seasons.

Sluggin' Sammy
Until 1998, the single-season record for homers was 61. Since then, Sosa has topped that mark three times, including a career-best 66 in 1998.

The hit parade goes on and on. Vladimir Guerrero of the Expos has been called one of the best all-around players in baseball. He combines great hitting with speed and a fantastic throwing arm. Vladimir's brother Wilton is also in the Majors.

Bueno!
Vladimir Guerrero had 100 or more RBI in six straight seasons.

Triple crown
Pedro Martinez accomplished a rare feat in 1999 and 2001. He won pitching's "triple crown" by leading the league in wins, strikeouts, and earned run average (ERA). ERA measures the average of how many runs a pitcher gives up in a game.

Shortstops from the Dominican Republic have always been special players. The island just seems to create fine-fielding players. Miguel Tejada of the Oakland A's is the latest in a long line of such players. He was the A.L. MVP in 2002.

Albert Pujols, the 2001 N.L. Rookie of the Year, has had two of the greatest seasons ever for a player just starting out. He plays several positions and is a top hitter.

Don't forget pitchers, either. Pedro Martinez has won three Cy Young Awards, including two in a row with the Boston Red Sox, and is perhaps the most feared pitcher in the league.

An island covered with waving palm trees, cooled by ocean breezes, and surrounded by beautiful sandy beaches is home to many of baseball's greatest players.

Original Cy
The Cy Young Award is named for a pitcher who won an all-time record 511 games during a career that lasted from 1890 to 1911.

His A game
After two solid seasons in 2000 and 2001, Miguel Tejada busted out in 2002, setting career highs in homers (34), RBI (131), and average (.308).

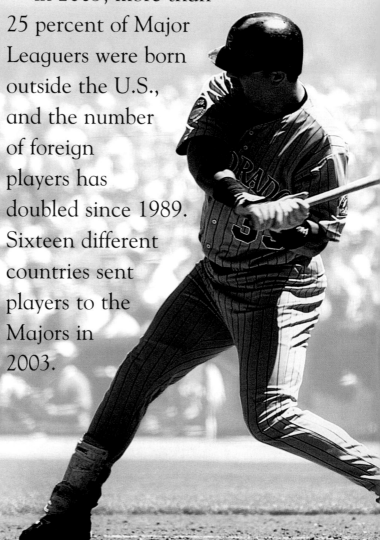

The rest of the world

The countries we have visited so far have produced the best and largest number of Major League players. But they are not the only places that Major Leaguers come from. In fact, in 2003, more than 25 percent of Major Leaguers were born outside the U.S., and the number of foreign players has doubled since 1989. Sixteen different countries sent players to the Majors in 2003.

Small country, big talent
The tiny Caribbean island of Curaçao is home to Andruw Jones of the Braves. Jones is one of baseball's best fielders.

O Canada!
Growing up in British Columbia, Larry Walker was a hockey star. But he was also pretty good at baseball and joined the Montreal Expos in 1989. In 1995, he moved to the Rockies.

Our neighbors to the north have sent players south for a century. In fact, in 1874, a team from Ontario, Canada, was the champion of the International League (a minor league one level down from the Majors).

Pitcher Ferguson Jenkins was from Ontario. In 1991, he became the first Canadian player to be named to the Baseball Hall of Fame.

Among current Canadian players, Eric Gagne is a standout. He became one of baseball's top closers by saving 52 games for the Dodgers in 2002.

Outfielder Larry Walker is perhaps Canada's best player ever. Walker has won three N.L. batting titles and six Gold Gloves. He was also the 1997 N.L. MVP. It's a good thing he chose baseball over a career in ice hockey!

Fergie
Durable pitcher Ferguson Jenkins was born in Ontario. He had a Hall of Fame career with four teams, winning 284 games.

Gold Gloves
Top fielders in both leagues at each position win this award for fielding excellence. Three outfielders from both leagues are named.

Different kind of South
The Korean pro league has improved a lot in recent years. Hee Seop Choi smacked enough homers in his home country to attract Major League scouts.

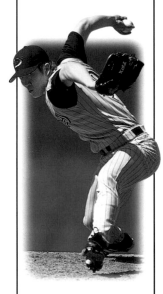

Sidearmer
Byung-Hyun Kim uses an unusual style of pitching. His sidearm delivery makes the ball hard for batters to spot.

Far away from chilly Canada is another country with long baseball roots. Australia was introduced to the game by American gold miners in 1874. Albert Spalding's tour in 1888 helped spread the game. (While Americans showed the locals how to throw a baseball, Australian aborigines demonstrated the boomerang to the visitors!)

Today, the nation hosts a professional league and has sent several players to the Majors, including pitcher Graeme Lloyd and catcher Dave Nilsson.

And Asian baseball is not just Japanese, either. Korea also has a pro league. From there, Chan Ho Park became the first Korean in the Majors when he joined the Dodgers in 1994. Byung-Hyun Kim helped Arizona win the 2001 World Series. And Cubs' first baseman Hee Seop Choi is the first position player in the Majors from Korea.

Park it
Chan Ho Park pitched for the Dodgers from 1994 to 2001 before moving over to the Texas Rangers in 2002. While with L.A., he put together four seasons with ERAs lower than 4.00.

43

Math time!
Rod Carew was one of baseball's top hitters. A player's hitting skill is measured by his batting average. To figure out a player's average, divide his total hits by his at-bats. For instance, in 1977, Rod had 239 hits in 616 at-bats. Divide 239 by 616 and you get an answer of .388. That was high enough to lead the American League.

Perfection
A pitcher, such as Dennis Martinez, throws a perfect game when he does not allow a single batter to reach base safely by any means.

Back in the Americas, many other countries in Central America and the Caribbean have produced top players. Panama's Rod Carew won seven A.L. batting titles.

Carew had 3,053 career hits, and is a member of the Baseball Hall of Fame.

Today's top Panamanian pitcher is reliever Mariano Rivera of the Yankees. In four World Series, Rivera set an all-time record with eight career saves.

Pitcher Dennis Martinez is so popular in his native Nicaragua that he is called "El Presidente" (The President). From 1977–1999, he was named to five All-Star teams and won 245 games. In 1990, he became one of only 16 pitchers in baseball history to throw a perfect game.

Today, Philadelphia pitcher Vicente Padilla of Nicaragua follows in Martinez's footsteps.

Dutch boy
Pitcher Bert Blyleven is one of only a few players to come to the Majors from the Netherlands.

Chili chillin'
Born in Jamaica, outfielder and designated hitter Chili Davis had a fine Major League career with several teams, including the Giants and the Angels.

D.C. baseball
A Major League team called the Senators played in the nation's capital from 1901 to 1971.

Young star
In the 2002 postseason, Francisco Rodriguez thrilled the baseball world by winning five games in relief. His great fastball earned him the nickname "K-Rod." K is the symbol for a strikeout.

Farther south, the South American nation of Venezuela has sent many fine players north to the U.S. The first was Chico Carrasquel in 1939 with the Washington Senators. In 2003, nearly 40 players on Major League rosters were from Venezuela.

Among them are Anaheim Angels World Series hero Francisco Rodriguez, Chicago White Sox slugger Magglio Ordonez, and Seattle Mariners ace Freddy Garcia.

Shortstop Omar Vizquel of Cleveland is also from Venezuela. His fielding skills helped him earn nine Gold Gloves, while his speed has made him a top basestealer.

Throughout the Major Leagues, in clubhouses from Los Angeles to Montreal, from Toronto to Atlanta, players from around the world are making a huge impact. Where will the next international superstars come from?

Well, I wonder if they play baseball on Mars. . . .

Great glove
Omar Vizquel has anchored the Cleveland Indians' infield since 1994, after playing for Seattle from 1989 to 1993.

Ice ball
No stars in this game of baseball played at the frozen South Pole!

Glossary

All-Star Game
An annual game played between the best players from the American and National Leagues.

American League (A.L.)
One of two groups of teams that make up Major League Baseball.

bunting
A batting skill that involves tapping the ball into play, usually in order to help a baserunner advance.

closer
A relief pitcher who specializes in getting the final outs of a close game.

commonwealth
A country that is governed locally but is voluntarily united with the United States.

delivery
A pitcher's motion in throwing the ball toward home plate.

designated hitter
In the American League only, the pitcher does not bat and teams use a player called this to bat in his place.

ERA
Stands for earned-run average, a measure of how many runs a pitcher gives up on average in every nine innings he pitches.

gets the sign
A term for a pitcher looking in toward a catcher, who is signaling with his fingers what pitch the pitcher should throw next.

Gold Gloves
Awards given to top fielders at each position in both leagues.

grand slam
A home run hit with the bases loaded.

legacy
Something left behind when something ends or someone dies.

Little League World Series
The annual championship of the internationl youth baseball league. The 11-12 year-old division championship is the most famous.

National League (N.L.)
One of two groups of teams that make up Major League Baseball.

Negro Leagues
Until 1947, African-American players were not allowed to play in the Major Leagues. The Negro Leagues were the only way that they could play pro baseball. "Negro" was an old term for African-Americans.

perfect game
A game in which the starting pitcher wins the game and does not allow a single batter to reach base safely.

pinch-hitter
A batter who takes the place of another batter in the batting order.

rookie
A player in his first season in Major League Baseball. (This term is used in other sports, too.)

roster
The list of players on a team.

socialist
A type of government that tries to distribute wealth equally among all people.

starting rotation
The group of pitchers who start games for a team. They usually work in the same order, game after game, during the season.

Index